Poems from
Pembrokeshire
Selected by Amy Wack

Seren is the book imprint of
Poetry Wales Press Ltd.
57 Nolton Street, Bridgend, Wales, CF31 3AE

www.serenbooks.com
facebook.com/SerenBooks
twitter@SerenBooks

ISBN: 978-1-78172-486-6

The publisher acknowledges the financial assistance of the Welsh Books Council.

Cover photograph: © Tim Hill / Tenby – Pixabay

Printed in the Czech Republic by Akcent Media Ltd.

Contents

Acknowledgements

We gratefully acknowledge the permission of the publishers of the titles from which these poems are taken:

Tony Curtis: 'Pembrokeshire Buzzards' from *Taken for Pearls*, (Seren, 1993); **Waldo Williams**: 'In Two Fields' translated by Tony Conran in *Welsh Verse*, (Seren reprint 2017); **Gillian Clarke**: 'Wild Orchids' from *Letting in the Rumour*, (Carcanet, 1989); **A.C. Bevan**: 'Effects of Weathering...' new poem; **Peter Finch**: 'Things in the Western Sky' from *Real Wales*, (Seren, 2008); **R.S. Thomas**: 'A Line from St. David's' from *The Bread of Truth*, (Rupert Hart-Davis, 1963); **Menna Elfyn**: 'St. Govan on the Eve of 2000' commissioned for S4c film where author appeared in St. Govan and recited poem, 2000; **Hilary Llewellyn-Williams**: 'What Brynach Saw' from *Animaculture*, (Seren, 1997); **Alison Bielski**: 'Boatman' from *Across the Burning Sand*, (Gomer,1970); **Ben Ray**: 'The Landsker Line' new poem; **Gwyneth Lewis**: 'The Voledom of Skomer' from *Parables and Faxes*, (Bloodaxe, 1995); **Rowan Williams**: 'Nevern Churchyard, The Bleeding Yew' from *The Other Mountain*, (Carcanet, 2014); **Philip Gross**: 'Prints' new poem; **Maggie Harris**: Part 1 from: 'On Watching a Lemon Sail the Sea' – entire long poem was prizewinner in the Welsh International Poetry Contest, 2017; **Duncan Bush**: 'Ramsey Island' from *Salt*, (Seren, 1985). (asking estate); **David Foster-Morgan**: 'Tenby Shores' appeared in earlier draft titled 'Sea Stones' in *Envoi*; **Br. David Hodges**: 'Caldey Island' from *Songs of Solitude* available at Caldey Island Bookshop; **Amy Wack**: 'Goscar Rock' new poem; **Matthew Francis**: 'The Assembly of the Noble Head' new poem – not included in his *Mabinogion* collection from Faber, 2017; **George Sandifer-Smith**: 'The Wreck of the Empress' new poem; **David Emrys James**: 'Horizon' translated by Tony Conran, *Welsh Verse*, (Seren); **Tiffany Atkinson**: 'Grassholm' from *Catulla Et Al*, (Bloodaxe, 2011); **Emily Hinshelwood**: 'Pwllcrochan' from *On Becoming a Fish*, (Seren, 2012); **David Emrys James**: 'Horizon' translated by Tony Conran in *Welsh Verse*, (Seren); **Wendy French**: 'Llawhaden House, Narberth' new poem; **Samantha Wynne-Rhydderch**: 'Snooker' new poem; **Tony Curtis**: 'Taken for Pearls' by Tony Curtis *From the Fortunate Isles: New and Selected Poems*, (Seren, 2016). (Thanks are due to Tony Curtis, also the Editor of *The Poetry of Pembrokeshire*, (Seren,1995).

Tony Curtis

PEMBROKESHIRE BUZZARDS

The buzzards of my boyhood days are back again,
their wide-stretched, ragged wings
like distant, emblematic kites. Our speed brings
them close to, still as icons, precisely drawn.

A single blown buzzard's egg nested in Pwllcrochan
at the centre of gull, wren and blackbird
in my shotgun-toting cousin's collection,
coffined in the shoe-box under his bed.

For twenty years since then, in my middle time,
they were rare. It seemed they had gone
the way of the plagued rabbits. The oily spew
of the refineries, the tourists' fumes

and farmers' chemicals had seen them off. But
now the buzzards of my growing years are back.
Each road, every deep, high-hedged track
is reigned over by a pair – imperious, vigilant.

Where did they go? All these years.
Somewhere unseen, perched high in pylons, poles and trees
their clawed, bobbing weight was riding always.
Above our speeding car, memories lift off the wires.

Waldo Williams

IN TWO FIELDS

Wewn Parc y Blawd and *Parc y Blawd* – two fields in Pembrokeshire

Where did the sea of light roll from
Onto Flower Meadow Field and Flower Field?
After I'd searched for long in the dark land,
The one that was always, whence did he come?
Who, oh who was the marksman, the sudden enlightener?
The roller of the sea was the field's living hunter.
From above bright-billed whistlers, prudent scurry of lapwings,
The great quiet he brought me.

Excitement he gave me, where only
The sun's thought stirred to lyrics of warmth,
Crackle of gorse that was ripe on escarpments,
Hosting of rushes in their dream of blue sky.
When imagination wakens, who calls
Rise up and walk, dance, look at the world?
Who is it hiding in the midst of the words
That were there on Flower Meadow Field and Flower Field?

And when the big clouds, the fugitive pilgrims,
Were red with the sunset of stormy November,
Down where the ashtrees and maples divided the fields,
The song of the wind was deep like deep silence,
Who, in the midst of the pomp, the super-abundance,
Stands there inviting, containing it all?
Each witness' witness, each memory's memory, life of each life,
Quiet calmer of the troubled self.

Till at last the whole world came into the stillness
And on the two fields his people walked,
And through, and between, and about them, goodwill widened
And rose out of hiding, to make them all one,
As when the few of us forayed with pitchforks
Or from heavy meadows lugged thatching of rush,
How close we came then, one to another –
The quiet huntsman so cast his net round us!

Ages of the blood on the grass and the light of grief,
Who whistled through them? Who heard but the heart?
The cheater of pride, and every trail's tracker,
Escaper from the armies, hey, there's his whistling –
Knowledge of us, knowledge, till at last we do know him!
Great was the leaping of hearts, after their ice age.
The fountains burst up towards heaven, till,
Falling back, their tears were like leaves of a tree.

Day brooks on all this beneath sun and cloud,
And Night through the cells of her wide-branching brain –
How quiet they are, and she breathing freely
Over Flower Meadow Field and Flower Field –
Keeps a grip on their object, the fields full of folk.
Surely these things must come. What hour will it be
That the outlaw comes, the hunter, the claimant to the breach,
That the Exiled King cometh, and the rushes part in his way?

translated by Tony Conran

7

Gillian Clarke

WILD ORCHIDS

Hot stink of orchid in the woods at Fforest.
Downstream of the waterfall I breathed
their scent and touched their purple towers,
the swollen root that cures the King's Evil
and makes the heart hot. Not flowers to share
to bring home for a jar.
Ophelia's long purples, tragic flowers.
You could believe they grew beneath the cross
and no amount of rain could wash the blood
from their stained leaves.

They called and called but I would not hear,
mixing their voices with waves and water.
Crouched in the blackthorn tunnel the cattle made
as they swayed their way to the sea, loosed
from the beudy by Gwilym and slapped free,
I was hooked on dens and secret places,
illicit books, visions and diaries
and the tomcat scent of orchids. Nothing
would fetch me but hunger, or the sound
of shadows stepping closer.

A.C. Bevan

EFFECTS OF WEATHERING ON IN SITU DOLERITE AND RHYOLITE OUTCROPS FROM THE PRESELI MOUNTAINS, SOUTH WALES

(Potts, Bernardini, Jones, et al.) X-Ray Spectrometry, December, 2005.

Exposure to the elements &
climate of Carn Menyn, on
rock samples of rhyolite &
igneous spotted dolerite blue–

stones, reveals depletion rates
in surface concentrations of
calcium & yttrium consistent
with a steady-state. Whilst

lead contents are markedly
increased due to emissions,
exhaust fumes & 'activities'
in step with ancient Britons

who hauled them down the A40
on their way to Cor y Cewri.

Peter Finch

THINGS IN THE WESTERN SKY

Buddha
Boundless
1024 millibars rising
Storm Cone
Skybolt
Cirrus
Saucer
West Minster migrant saint
Shed of air
The western skies are full of
Vapour crimson (why?) shards of ice
(delete shard) sheds of ice (substitute crisp)
Crisp shatter
Light full of translucent altocumulous
Shape of bone hoard
(add hymn)
Jehovah
Guide me
Pull me on

Sky full of rain

Sky full of light

R.S. *Thomas*

A LINE FROM ST. DAVID'S

I am sending you this letter,
Something for neo-Edwardians
Of a test-tube age to grow glum about
In their conditioned libraries.
As I came here by way of Plwmp,
There were hawkweeds in the hedges:
Nature had invested all her gold
In the industry of the soil.
There were larks, too, like a fresh chorus
Of dew, and I thought, remembering Dewi
The water-drinker, the way back
Is not so far as the way forward.
Here the cathedral's bubble of stone
Is still unpricked by the mind's needle,
And the wall lettuce in the crevices
Is as green now as when Giraldus
Altered the colour of his thought
By drinking from the Welsh fountain...

I ramble; what I wanted to say
Was that the day has a blue lining
Partly of sky, partly of sea;
That the old currents are in the grass,
Though rust has becalmed the plough.
Somewhere a man sharpens a scythe:
A child watches him from the brink
Of his own speech, and this is of more
Importance than all the visitors keeping
A spry saint asleep in his tomb.

Menna Elfyn

ST GOVAN ON THE EVE OF 2000

So where will I be on the day of celebration
when the new age sparkles but seek solitude?
Where history lies locked
in the depths as water-drops praise
the ancient music over strings
in the rock of the well's treasure chest.

Go like the mute to the rim of St *Gofan*,
the sunset a fire in my hands,
gaze towards the horizon, how
over the sea's turbulence
the world's currents gather drumming.

Here tide and time weigh us in their scale;
the eight thousand waves that daily break in chorus,
where the sea's tongues bell and burble.

Here *plygain*'s three blessings of welcome:
water for the thirsty from the well's cup,
refuge for the weary as they reach ashore,
a hearth of hollow wood to warm the soul.
Easy to forget in this rock-womb
a world drowning in ashes and baubles,
in our brief tenantry here, waves wallowing
as ever, between 'croes' and *croeso*.

translated by Gillian Clarke and the poet

★ *croes*, cross & *croeso*, welcome
★ *plygain*: matins– from Latin: cock's crow

Hilary Llewellyn-Williams

WHAT BRYNACH SAW

Carn Ingli, Pembrokeshire

Someone saw angels on this hill.
One of those early saints, the tough
weathered sort with big hands
and knotty calf-muscles; the wild-eyed
sort gazing into a grey gale,
cloak bucking around him; rough
jowled, broken toothed from an old brawl
those nights before he fell in love
with the sky and became a saint.

A youth spent handling cattle,
hacking at stumps, cutting peat in the rain
to stack in low skewed rows
for the wind to dry. Planting beans, stooped
to earth; wrestling a boar down
for gelding in the swamp of the yard;
the screams, the stink, the swearing.
Brynach. A lad with a dusk thirst
no cask of ale could kill.

Parched, he longed to drink light
in bellyfuls, to feel clouds
surge through him. Watched swifts
dart and skim, watched the kite
hover. Fledged in the new religion,
discovered heaven as the mountaintops
sliced into his mind: dark blades
of ice, slipped scree. Here he stepped free
from flesh, from that long battle.

Alone with his love, arms out
to the sun like a heathen, he felt
the wind lift and hold him aloft
like the breath of God. From this height
the world is beautiful. You can carry it
all in your hands, the little stonewalled fields,
the sea leaping. You can see
what Brynach saw; how angels in the hill
raise their stone wings for flight.

Alison Bielski

BOATMAN

Boatman, in a rain of spray, comes
Cockle treading in salt-faded shoes
Eyes blue mussel shells, white lined
(sight keen as an east wind)
A being more of sea than land

Escorted by noisy gull outriders
He patrols his tide-edge kingdom
Nodding at boats, bell lobster pots
Ropes twisted on driftwood shore
King of the ebb-tide pacing out
His realm through kneeling waves

Ben Ray

THE LANDSKER LINE

The Landsker Line is a term used for the distinct linguistic and cultural boundary between the Welsh speaking areas of northern Pembrokeshire and the English speaking areas of southern Pembrokeshire, an area known as 'Little England beyond Wales'.

Tread softly. The Landsker Line runs through this place,
cutting you straight down the tongue
plucking vocal chords to different rhythms.
This is war on a geographical scale. Watch-tower words
crouch in map folds, consonants drawn –
and underneath, language forces earth together
in a border crossing of flint-filled, igneous Cymraeg
pushed up against English's softer sedimentary curves.
Put the dictionary down, there is no escape.
In Newgale the frontier carves a village in half,
Brandy Brook an anglicised battle line
the next beach north a fighting statement: Pen-y-Cwm.
To trace it you will need a phrasebook
and the voice of your grandfather – time clots
and cloys in the breaths between sentences.
Norman castles were scattered like leftover thoughts
Roch, Llawhaden, Narberth, as if thrown up in haste
to hold back these strange beasts of burden
two voices that speak from the same body.
Tomorrow, as you ebb and wash on inland waves
memories of dissonant echoes will still ring in the ears –
thin line drawn over the voice of your mother tongue
Little England beyond Wales, Sir Benfro Saesneg.

Gwyneth Lewis

THE VOLEDOM OF SKOMER

For thirty years a suburban naturalist
has studied the life of the SKOMER VOLE
as a pattern of rodent parochial.
His colleagues consider him a purist,
look down on his subject as insular,
but he's entranced by the phenomena of local
and all things SKOMER are his exotica.

He's made a fetish of specificity:
the Ramsey field vole's all very well
and yes, he quite likes the pipistrelle,
but the SKOMER VOLE? – Passionate loyalty
and an endless interest in the ins and outs
of a vole that is wholly residual,
one that missed, as it were, the mainland boat

And, surrounded by water, took a snack and just stayed.
In secret he cherishes a mythic version:
the Ur-Vole, a Moses, leads an excursion
across the causeway on a vole crusade
down the slopes of the slippery Continental Shelf
to Skomer and visionary seclusion,
to the safety of his supernatural self.

In the field he's a hawk-eyed devotee,
finding births, deaths and couplings a revelation
for one man's life spans many generations
of SKOMER VOLE nations and dynasties.
He stoops like a question while, above him, the sky
tries in vain to touch his imagination;
clouds on their columns of rain pass him by,

for he's not drawn to the world by grandeur
but by hours of waiting for the lash of a tail,
for that blur in the dune grass that might be a male.
No, he's wooed through his voleish sense of wonder,
tied by attention to a piece of land
that he feels, one evening, might just set sail
for its observant and most loving husband.

Rowan Williams

NEVERN CHURCHYARD,
THE BLEEDING YEW

Sliced clean as marble; the glassy mourner
bending to read the blunt letters, the routines
of leavetaking. But glass will splinter: ragged bites
stand open and the port-red ooze, crusted
like scale in kettles, wanders, slow as a winter fly,
across the arctic slope. Gashed bodies
push out their sickness through the skin:
the marble mourner has leached up the fevers
from the rubbed lives around its roots,
sucking the moisture of the leaf-choked, rust-throated
fountain forgotten in the wood, the well
of loss, wounds, endings, seeping out
under the prosaic stones, clouding the glass,
cracking the ice. The tree of discharge.

Philip Gross
PRINTS

for Mike Perry: Flip-flops and Shoes, part of the Môr Plastig project, a photographic study of plastic objects washed up along the Welsh coastline

a)   On beach after beach, at tideline after tideline, it is the sole that survives, its flimsy uppers rotted. You could think the sea was attempting a pun, as well as theology.

b)   To step is... a step. It has (it thinks) direction. Then the sea gets to work, turns it thiswhichway and that. Or sometimes upside downs, as if it should at least consider the ground's point of view.

c)   For several centuries the Buddha was not represented, not by a face or a posture – just a footprint. One. And already vacated. True likeness of his absence, carved in rock.

d)   We would so like to think that our steps in the sand were like fingerprints, uniquely us. Ask the sea, as it gathers and wipes the data with each tide. It doesn't compute.

e)   This flipflop, with the sand and shell adhering, or the trainer sole that melts a little to digest a little of the beach... they seem to be preparing, like a caddis larva in its case, to become something new.

f)   Other soles become the maps, as they decay, of their own journeys – here's one back into deep time, look, here's Gondwanaland, in case you you ever need to go.

g)   Just south of the Olduvai Gorge, two adults, and a child between them... They may be fleeing, as the ash falls round them, preserving their prints. Yes, Australopithecus walks, as we do. 3.7 million years ago. Already, now and then, the child turns to look back.

Maggie Harris

FROM: ON WATCHING A LEMON SAIL THE SEA

I set you free
to take to the sea again
on a high tide, with breakers rushing the beach
like warriors.
They pummel the sand, scythe
a four foot chasm into the mouth
of a lonely river
beat the rocks' submerged heads
batter the cliffs again
                    and again
                              and again

The sea, beyond its charge was waiting –
a winter morning sea, a Twelfth Night sea
tumultuous and moody
                    waiting

A strange gift, you
a large, perfect lemon
fresh and sharp as the sun-birght
wind-cut winter's day. But I
unsure of your heritage
refused you.

Duncan Bush

RAMSEY ISLAND

Drab gorse crouches;
and the stunted thorn, its back bent
from the lash, fleeing
the wind-
but root-bound,
like the girl becoming laurel.

There are no nymphs or gods pursuant
here;
barely a crippled tree is bared
against the sky.

Only wind, running
the turf one way like a close pelt;
and precipices to the sea.

Even men, who root anywhere,
landed, lasted a few brute seasons out,
were gone.
There is nothing to grip on.

★

The island's a bird sanctuary now.
Like the leaning wind, it has
prevailed,
becoming finally what it always was.

The once-gutted stone
habitation has been renovated for the warden.
With his deep-freeze, radio and books,
his sinecure's
as steady as a lighthouse job.

He'll last here longer than those
who had to, and couldn't –
each crude, repetitive meal
earned
singly, eaten
after darkness off the day's bare plate –

the fish-taste of gull-eggs;
a rim of chipped bone.

★

Cut-off in winter
for weeks at a stretch, you hunched to stare across
the straits and see
a man ploughing a field dark
on the mainland in a cloud of gulls,
as if on the next hill.

Here on the dirt was
thinner than the scalp on your skull.

But there were worse straits –
the rock was
fast;
you thought of those out in that running sea.

A fine day
was not a respite but increase of labour.

Yet there were the moments going
out at morning;
the sea sometimes when the back straightened.

In a bleak, intermittent
diary, kept a full year he survived
on the island, Ivor Arnold, poor
at spelling, and grudging
his entries
like flour or paraffin or twine,
recorded of a day in March, 1908.

'Wind S. A fine day. I could hear
Will Morris Pencarnan talking
to his horses yesterday from Congrwn Bach.'

David Foster-Morgan

TENBY SHORES

I shuck the first oyster, unlock
two coasts: a kelp-walled harbour, pooling
November ocean; and in cameo
a sepia beach deserted at dawn.

They prick and barb, test the thickness of my skin,
the top-shells hard as seven hundred tides,
an alluvium at the hinge,
dirt spotted with cobalt and garnet.

Conch-bottomed they balance, smelling of life
and metal, five rock pools on the plate.
A strong tongue in each of them,
slugs of salt churned to milky flesh.

David Hodges

CALDEY ISLAND

Battered by wind
and battered by sea,
only a fool would visit,
or make plans,
on an island
where the boats
are all 'Weather Permitting'.

No good to man
nor beast,
fit only for monks
and for prayer,
when the wind
is gale force
east-south-east.

Only a saint
would visit
in winter.

Amy Wack

GOSCAR ROCK

Talismanic, this giant rock,
this beast of slabs and fissures,

a stone shipwrecked on the north shore
long before the Viking who named it

stepped forth from a long boat
on his way to harrying the bishoprics,

planted his boots in the sand,
and gave it guttural twin syllables.

Gos-car. In its tilting layers read
epochs: those slates, packed mud

from the Jurassic, quartz seams:
limestone laid down in the Cretaceous.

You have to go back to the last ice age
to find the glacier enamoured enough

to sweep a hill off its feet, set it adrift
in the churning ice floes of the channel,

to cast it here, in the sand crescent
beneath cliff-nests of gulls and cormorants.

It seems almost impossible for walkers
to walk around it and not stop once

to touch its barnacled hide for luck,
to admire the neon-green of its lichens

before the tides do their diurnal work
and engulf its stone skirts in surf.

Matthew Francis

THE ASSEMBLY OF THE NOBLE HEAD

I
Two of the hall's doors are open. One gives on to fields,
a shifting pattern of cows. Grass and dung smells
sometimes creep in, but no noise or wind.
It never occurs to them
to close it, or leave.

Through the second a rectangle of ocean
is endlessly repainting itself
with brushes of rain and sun
and textures of black.

They are at a long table, laughing.
The giant's head laughs with them,
but won't eat or drink.

Behind it is a third door
they mustn't open.

II
Night blinks unnoticed in the doorways: no need to sleep
when every day's a dream. The yolk of the sun
slides across the sky and breaks in blood,
and no one stops his singing
or crosses himself.

There are ten fingers of air to play the harp,
footsteps and rustling to fill the cups.
The laughter dies down in time
to retell the joke,

and the wine's always at its zenith,
leaving no shadowy ache
to darken the brain.

The snows that flicker outside
can't whiten their hair.

III

Sometimes a man laughs till he gets a stitch in the mind
and there's no room to breathe, so he thinks instead,
and in that gasp glimpses a desire.
His hand may be on the door
before he forgets.

But one day he is playing with the doorlatch
and feels a singing under his hand,
a bullying charge of wind.
He swings it open

on a sea of sharp edges and sun,
the distant blur of Cornwall.
The room fills with cold

and fire and horses and blood,
and eighty lost years.

from the legend of the *Mabinogi:* The seven companions are taking the head
of Bendigeidfran to London but are enchanted for 80 years until one of them
opens the door and the spell is broken.

George Sandifer-Smith

THE WRECK OF THE EMPRESS

Skinned my feet and shins/
at St. Ann's Head
where I fell sideways/20:07.

Cargo/national lifeblood
ran from my wounds, starboard.
The operation made it worse/torn
torn torn/the tugs
letting go/over, over.

Filled the water/one
in three. 21:18/aground.
A thousand shells/poisoned/
drying/black seaweed.
Cockles/rockpools choking/
slick sticky unflying guillemots.

I was resurrected five times
over/a Milford Haven exile/
Third Wind/scars not visible
except for Pembrokeshire/the trim
on the rocks/my double decade shadow.

David Emrys James

HORIZON

Look, a mirage, like a round rim, a strange
    Wizard's masterpiece about us:
An old line that's not there,
A boundary that never ends.

translated by Tony Conran

27

Tiffany Atkinson

GRASSHOLM

The magic of one of the world's largest gannet colonies, close up
— Pembrokeshire Boat Charters

When the gannets turned her flesh
into a gannet, all the light blew in
at once. It sucked her skyward, shrieking.

He squinted from the stunned deck.
She was wheeling like a sycamore-
key. He had witnessed childbirth,

and the invisibility of pain, here,
too, was hurtful. Her mother's name
was what she cried out last. But chaos

mends. Then there she was, all china-curve
and braced wing, and a beak he thought
unusually expressive. He ran cold fingers

down her spine and knew the bones. Thrilled
with the common speech of touch, they spoke
in elemental terms that he would later publish

to acclaim. He passes seasons by himself
and reads the Mabinogion and Ovid. Calm
surprises him. He comes home from long visits

in the summer months with eyes like rock-pools.
She'll have given him Sistines of seabirds,
plummeting parabolas of love. And he'll

Have oiled and preened her feathers and her
blue feet – though it makes him faint, to feel
the quickfire of her heart and breathe the ocean

of her. Change like that must ruin ordinary
folk. These two far from ordinary, neither
knows who gained the greater freedom by it.

Emily Hinshelwood

PWLLCROCHAN

Jetties are matchsticks, balanced into piers.
Like card houses, eventually you stack one too many.

A tanker is docking three hundred thousand tons of oil,
ribbed waves rock to shore. Chimneys are belching,
a low hum under the pylon. The air smells of engine.

Everything crackles. Even the trees.
Out of a sycamore, a squirrel plummets
with a loud crack on the tarmac.

In the bay, a single turbine
spins, dizzy with the wind.

Wendy French

LLAWHADEN HOUSE, NARBERTH

i.m. Edith Thomas, step-grandmother

We'll never know about the fire that took
her life and burned the manor to the ground.

Some say it was a two-bar electric, others claim theories
of their own. Llawhaden, once the house we'd never dreamt

of entering, almost belonged to us. In *The Western Mail*
she's smiling in that battered hat she wore so well after Tadcu

had died. Llawhaden. The name rolled off our tongues like rhyme
as we followed Edith round to hear her talking to the cows,

helped to collect eggs and listened to her on the Bethesda organ.
The house with two staircases that led us up into the eaves, higher

than we'd ever been before. The house where Cromwell stayed.
Llawhaden. Stories of how he walked at night. We believed

her every word. His smile. His helmet. We doubted nothing.
We count the steps of disappearing, how she crept upstairs to bed

in that old familiar way. Which staircase?
On summer days in certain light she comes to mind.

Samantha Wynne-Rhydderch

SNOOKER

The table was tempting, the man went on to recount,
insulated in baize as it was, a second skin. It stretched

like a field whose boundary he could barely make out
being but eight at the time, and less than the height

of the snooker cue brooding in a corner of the day room
at Falcolndale Hall, a home for the elderly

who gripped the arms of chairs too deep to get out of
without help. The lad had been longing to pot

all of the balls corralled into a triangle and set off an echo
of blue, red and yellow like footsteps running back down

the lane to farmyards and stable doors whose latches
the old folks would've fastened before walking towards

broken lattices of porches they'd been intending to repair,
waltzing across flagstones to make their own tea.

Tony Curtis

TAKEN FOR PEARLS

In muddied waters the eyes of fishes
are taken for pearls.

As those two trout, little bigger than my hand then,
taken by spinner at Cresselly on an early

summer's day in the quiet afternoon
before the season's traffic. Only

a tractor in an unseen field
stitching the air like a canopy over it all.

And the taste of them pan-fried nose to tail
by my mother. The sweet flesh prised from

cages of the most skilfully carved bone.
I closed my eyes and she smiled for me.